GONE WITH THE GIN

GONE WITH THE GIN

COCKTAILS WITH A HOLLYWOOD TWIST

TIM FEDERLE

ILLUSTRATED BY LAUREN MORTIMER

RUNNING PRESS
PHILADELPHIA · LONDON

© 2015 by Tim Federle
Illustrations © by Lauren Mortimer

Published by Running Press,
A Member of the Perseus Books Group

Printed in China

Books published by Running Press are available at special discounts for bulk purchases
in the United States by corporations, institutions, and other organizations. For more
information, please contact the Special Markets Department at the Perseus Books
Group, 2300 Chestnut Street, Suite 200, Philadelphia, PA 19103, or call
(800) 810-4145, ext. 5000, or e-mail special.markets@perseusbooks.com.

ISBN 978-0-7624-5860-8
Library of Congress Control Number: 2015934573

E-book ISBN 978-0-7624-5864-6

9 8 7 6 5 4 3 2
Digit on the right indicates the number of this printing

Cover and interior design by Josh McDonnell
Edited by Jordana Tusman
Consulting bartender: Cody Goldstein
Typography: Artisan, Avenir, Lato, and Splandor

Running Press Book Publishers
2300 Chestnut Street
Philadelphia, PA 19103-4371

Visit us on the web!
www.offthemenublog.com

This book is dedicated to Jordana Tusman,
the movie star of book editors.

Coming Attractions

Introduction

Here's drinking with you, kid

Attention, Film Buffs:

We know your type. You've seen *Star Wars* so many times, you're basically half-Jedi. You love the smell of napalm in the morning, you see dead people, and you're the king (or queen!) of the world. Hell, you can't even walk *past* a box of chocolates without quoting *Forrest Gump*. You've basically logged more hours at the local megaplex than the projectionist—and you deserve a drink! But hold on, Butch Cassidy. A Diet Coke and Milk Duds isn't gonna cut it. Not tonight.

To give a red carpet–worthy welcome to history's most famous films, we've meticulously mixed a mouthwatering assortment of tipsy tributes so diverse and wide-ranging, you could line the shelves of an abandoned Blockbuster with these drinks—twice. Included within are scholarly sips for cinephiles, if you will—and the people who love them. From mixologists to moviegoers, welcome to *Gone with the Gin: Cocktails with a Hollywood Twist*. Please, find a seat on the aisle (preferably one with a cup holder) and silence your cell phones.

No matter your cinematic stripe, there's a beverage (or ten) tailor-made just for you. For those morose moviegoers who never leave the house without Kleenex, get ready to cry-slash-chug your way through history's most delectable dramas. From A Sidecar Named Desire to Ti-tonic, this section packs a major emotional picture punch.

Craving something a tad bubblier? Turn to You've Got Ale, Some Spike It Hot, or Monty Python and the Stoli Grail, if you'd rather cackle than cry. We go from rom-com to rowdy in our silliest section.

Perhaps you'd prefer your sips chilling and your pics thrilling. You're covered, too, with The French Concoction, The Moon-Shining, and a host of other devilish drinks that you'll call scary-good.

And if you like your cocktails sprinkled with song, Bloody Mary Poppins and Little Schnapps of Horrors will have you dancing out of your seat—for another round.

Not to worry, Trekkies over twenty-one: If your favorite thing on earth is to leave the planet, you'll swear you were abducted after sampling our frothy fantasies and sip-worthy sci-fi section. (Close Encounters of the Slurred Kind, anyone?)

Of course, no trip to the movies would be complete without a stop at the concession stand! If your popcorn's gone by the time previews are over, stay tuned for The Silence of the Lamb Burgers, The Breakfast Cereal Club, and a star-studded roster full of other movie munchies.

For those viewers who can't tell their *Dirty Harry* from their dirty martini, first up is a breezy crash course on the tools, techniques, and terms used throughout this book. And on those nights when you and your friends finally pick a flick, shut down your devices and pull out our drinking games—if, that is, you're brave enough to "take a shot every time somebody says the f-word in *Pulp Fiction*."

So go ahead, make my drink. Even if you don't know every line from every movie, tonight you're gonna drink like you do.

TOOLS

GLASSWARE

Cocktail (or martini) glass (4 to 6 ounces): Drinks are shaken and strained into this iconic long-stemmed, V-shaped beauty.

Collins glass (10 to 14 ounces): Best for very large, icy tropical drinks, a Collins glass is built like a highball glass, but taller and narrower.

Copper mug (16 to 20 ounces): This traditional serving glass for the Moscow Mule is not essential to a well-stocked home bar, but is certainly a high-style addition.

Flute (4 to 6 ounces): Champagne cocktails are served in this specially designed stemware, which showcases the bubbles without letting too many of them fly free.

Highball glass (10 to 12 ounces): This one is midway between a rocks and a Collins glass, but taller than the former and shorter and fatter than the latter.

Mason jar (1 cup to ½ gallon): Though generally used for bottling preserves, this also makes a great container for casual drinks.

Mug (10 to 12 ounces): The hardworking coffee cup does double-duty for hot alcoholic drinks.

Pint glass (16 to 20 ounces): An all-purpose beer-chugger, this glass tapers at the bottom. Some have a "bulb" near the lip for a better grip.

Rocks (or lowball or old-fashioned) glass (6 to 10 ounces): A drink poured "on the rocks"—that's over ice, rookie—is frequently served in one of these short, heavy tumblers.

Shot glass (¾ to 2 ounces): For enjoying a variety of aptly named "shots," this smallest of drinking vessels also comes in handy as a measuring device.

EQUIPMENT

Jigger: For small liquid measurements, this hourglass-shaped, metal tool is available in a variety of sizes. We prefer the 1-ounce-over-1½-ounces model—but do opt for a larger size if you're trying to get through *The Ten Commandments*. And just drink straight from the bottle if you're attempting the *Hobbit* trilogy.

Juicer: The classy crowd prefers their lemons and limes freshly juiced, whether by hand or by machine—but we won't balk if you go the bottled route. On average, lemons and limes produce about an ounce of juice each.

Measuring cups and spoons: Dry cups typically range from ¼ cup to 1 cup. For larger liquid measurements, it's easiest to have a standard 2-cup glass. Measuring spoons go from ¼ teaspoon to 1 tablespoon.

Mesh strainer: This small device is like a fine colander for drinks, and is used in recipes for which "double straining" is required for an extra-smooth pour.

Muddler: This is the grown-up term for a fruit masher and looks like a mini baseball bat. It releases oils and flavors in mints and berries.

Shaker: This is an essential device for creating James Bond–style martinis. Our fave is the *Cobbler*: a three-part (counting the capped lid) metal contraption with the strainer built right in. The other varieties are the *Boston* (which has a glass mixing cup and metal container) and the *French* (which is basically a Cobbler shaker sans the strainer). Both require a separate strainer, and that's valuable time you could be watching movies—or drinking—or both.

Strainer: This is like a sifter for liquids. If you ignored our advice to buy the all-in-one Cobbler shaker, you'll want to pick up a Hawthorne strainer, which should fit tightly into your shaker's metal mouth. The Hawthorne filters only the liquids (not the ice) into a cocktail.

Vegetable peeler (or channel knife): A handy shortcut for creating twists (see: Garnishes, page 18), a peeler removes a thin layer of skin from fruit, which you can use to add flavor and color.

ᵀECHNIQUES

MAKING A DRINK

Double straining: For some of the recipes, you'll need to hold a mesh strainer over the mouth of the glass and "double strain" the drink from the shaker through a strainer and *then* through the mesh, which makes for an ultra-clean pour.

Dry shaking: This is essentially the same as "Shaking" (page 18), but without the addition of ice to the shaker.

Dumping: After shaking your ingredients, you uncap the shaker and "dump" all that's inside—including, generally, the ice—as opposed to straining through a filter.

Filling: In some of the recipes, you're asked to "fill" your glass to the top with a final ingredient—typically Champagne, soda, or cream. The amount of liquid needed depends on how large your glass is.

Muddling: In some recipes, once you've filled a glass with the specified fruits, juices, or herbs, you will use a muddler (page 15) to gently mash the ingredients, twisting lightly to release their oils and flavors.

Rimming: This technique entails rubbing the lip of a glass with a lemon or lime wedge, then placing it upside down on a plate of salt, Tang powder, sugar, or whatever the recipe calls for. Gently rotate the glass so the rim gets coated in the desired ingredient.

Shaking: Fill a shaker tin with all of the ingredients and ice, cap shut, and shake vigorously—probably harder than you think— by holding the device over your shoulder and shaking for approximately ten seconds. (For egg-white cocktails, shake until the liquid takes on a foamy quality, or at least ten seconds.) Uncap the lid and strain (or "Dump," page 17) into a glass.

Stirring: Experts use a bar spoon, which has a long, twisting handle, but an everyday cereal spoon will do just fine. For cocktails with carbonation, the bubbles will do the stirring for you.

DECORATING A DRINK

Garnishes: Technically, a *garnish* adds both color and flavor (like a lime wedge or a lemon twist); *garbage* is any food or fruit that's solely for aesthetic purposes (like a lemon wheel); and *kitsch* is something hokey (like an umbrella, or the entire John Waters oeuvre). For our purposes, if it's not a liquid ingredient, we'll call it a "garnish" throughout.

Garnish techniques include:

Grating: This isn't just for cheese! Gently rub the ingredient in question (lemon peel, ginger) against the fine edge of a grater.

Twists: These delicately flavor a drink and add a little citrus pizzazz. The official method involves a channel knife, which peels a long, thin gouge out of a lemon. Our easier, preferred method is to wash a lemon and then use a vegetable peeler to remove a 2-inch strip of skin. Fold the strip in half, twist it over the drink, wipe the rim of the glass with the twist, and then drop it into the glass.

Wedges: This is the most widely used lemon or lime garnish. Wash, dry, and cut the ends off the whole fruit. Then chop the fruit in half "the short way," and quarter the remaining halves. Wedges can either be squeezed and dropped into the drink, or balanced on the rim after cutting a notch into the fruit.

Wheels: To make these circular discs of fruits or vegetables, wash, dry, and cut the ends off the whole fruit, then slice crosswise into "wheels," which can be placed in the drink, or balanced on the rim after cutting a notch into the fruit.

TERMS

SPIRITS

Brandy: Generally a distillation of wine or fruit juice; we also feature cognac, a type of brandy named for the town in France—and endorsed by none other than Martin Scorsese.

Gin: Distilled from grain and can be flavored with everything from juniper to cinnamon. Figures prominently in *Casablanca*.

Mezcal: Think of this as the smoky cousin of tequila, made from the Mexican maguey plant.

Rum: The best sugar water money can buy. The lightest kinds are the youngest; the darkest can be older than seven years. Johnny Depp kept a veritable "diary" of the stuff.

Tequila: Cue Pee-wee Herman in a biker bar. "Tequila!" comes from the blue agave plant, not the cactus. The word *tequila* itself refers to a region in Mexico, and the authentic stuff doesn't harbor any wayward worms.

Vodka: There'd be no *Big Lebowski* without vodka, because there'd be no White Russians. Odorless and clear, vodka is typically distilled from potatoes and grains.

Whiskey: A broad term that includes bourbon and rye; distilled from grains and hailing from America, Canada, Ireland, or Scotland. Most important? Whiskey is the spirit Bill Murray promotes in *Lost in Translation*.

LIQUEURS AND APERITIFS

These are strong, syrupy spirits that are flavored any number of ways, from fruits to flowers; also includes schnapps. The following liqueurs make appearances throughout: *bitter orange* (brands like Campari and Aperol); *Caribbean blends* (a generic like Falernum); *citrus blends* (a brand like Lillet); *coffee* (a brand like Kahlúa); *crème de banane* (banana flavor); *crème de cacao* (chocolate flavor); *crème de menthe* (mint flavor); *crème de pêche* (peach flavor); *crème de violette* (violet flavor); *elderflower*; *ginger* (a brand like Domaine de Canton); *herbal liqueurs* (generics like amaro; brands like Bénédictine, Galliano, and Green Chartreuse); *honey liqueur* (a brand like Drambuie); *Irish coffee* (a brand like Baileys); *lavender*; *licorice* (a generic like Pastis); *maraschino cherry* (a brand like Luxardo); *orange* (generics like triple sec and curaçao; brands like Cointreau and Grand Marnier); and *raspberry*.

BEER

Beer is practically a supporting character in *Dazed and Confused*. Recipes in this book focus on ales (generally bitter and fruity) and stouts (generally dark and heavy).

WINE

Fermented juice from myriad fruits and grapes. In subcategories, we feature: *Champagne*, a sparkling white wine from a specific French region; *pinot noir*, a popular, slightly temperamental-to-produce type of red wine; *port*, generally a red dessert wine produced in a specific region of Portugal; *Prosecco*, sort of like Champagne's Italian cousin, though produced in a different way and with a sweeter finish; *sherry*, a fortified beverage produced in Spain using white grapes; *shiraz*, a popular red wine that originated in France and has been perfected in Australia; and *sweet vermouth*, a fortified wine flavored with herbs.

OTHER FLAVORINGS

Agave nectar: A widely available sweetener, it goes down like honey with an exotic accent.

Bitters: This cologne of cocktails is added in small amounts to give a drink depth and nuance. Those featured in this book range from chocolate mole to baked apple to the more standard Angostura bitters.

Brandied cherries: The maraschino cherry's sophisticated big sister is a cinch to make at home.

BRANDIED CHERRIES

Place ½ pound sweet (destemmed) cherries and 1 or 2 vanilla beans in an uncapped glass jar and set aside. Gently heat 1 cup brandy and ½ cup sugar over low heat in a saucepan until the sugar is dissolved, and then pour the heated liquid into the jar. Cap the jar with a tight lid and shake the jar once per day, letting it sit for 2 weeks to a month, ideally in a sunny spot. Move to a dark location after opening, and enjoy within 9 months.

Cardamom: Favored in many Indian dishes, cardamom is one of the most expensive spices, by weight—but a little goes a long, memorable way.

Celery salt: This combination of two everyday ingredients lifts Bloody Marys to new heights.

Clove studs: The flowering bud of a type of evergreen tree is primarily used here in homey, hot cocktails.

Cream of coconut: If those 1960s beach party movies could be bottled, they'd taste like this sweetened coconut product (a brand like Coco Reàl) for tropical drinks.

Grain alcohol: This liquid is pure and potent, containing almost twice the alcohol content of ordinary spirits. Use extremely sparingly.

Grenadine: This sweet red syrup is a snap to make—and loads better than the corporate high-fructose junk sold to bars.

GRENADINE SYRUP

Boil 2 cups bottled pomegranate juice (a brand like POM Wonderful) with 2 cups granulated sugar in a medium saucepan. Stir for 5 minutes, until it's reduced to half the original volume, into a syrup. Bottle and keep in the fridge for up to 3 weeks.

Lychee juice: This sweet, vitamin-and-potassium-packed juice comes from the Chinese lychee fruit.

Maraschino cherries: These bright red, artificially dyed cherries populate Shirley Temples and piña coladas.

Orange blossom water: This liquid comes from the distillation of bitter orange flowers.

Rose water: Rose petals are steeped in water to produce this delicately perfumed, delicious water.

Simple syrup: Avoid the high-fructose junk bottled by the gallon.

SIMPLE SYRUP

For easy, at-home simple syrup, boil 1 part water to 2 parts sugar, until it reduces to—you guessed it—syrup. Bottle, refrigerate, and enjoy within a month.

Star anise pod: This small, eight-segment spice pod offers a delicious licorice tang.

Thirsty yet?

These drinks aren't going to make themselves.

DRAMAS

"Of all the gin joints in all the towns in all the world, she walks into mine."

—Humphrey Bogart (as Rick Blaine) in *Casablanca*

Cue the violins and pick out your Oscars gown: We're gonna make you a cocktail you can't refuse. Our heavy-hitting hooch recipes complement the epic, tear-jerking, ship-sinking dramas that inspired them—an artful blend of modern-day masterpieces and black-and-white wonders. Have no fear: The flicks may be long and heavy, but the drinks go down quick and easy. Prepare to win Best Supporting Bartender after the credits stop rolling.

TEQUILA SUNRISE BOULEVARD

SUNSET BOULEVARD (1950) DIRECTED BY BILLY WILDER

In the days before social media in a pre-Photoshopped world, aging stars would drift into the background of their own minds and never be heard from again. These true-life Hollywood horror stories fascinated auteur Billy Wilder, who offered an ultra-dark look at the ultra-sunny Sunset Boulevard, specifically the glamorous and gilded Beverly Hills block on which former film beauty Norma Desmond's mansion sits in decadent disarray. When a downtrodden young screenwriter wanders up her driveway after escaping his own demons, Norma sees him as her chance at a comeback (even if *he* ends up seeing the bottom of the pool). Descend the staircase for a poolside-worthy poison featuring a (Pinot) noir twist.

1¾ ounces tequila

2 ounces orange juice

½ ounce Pinot Noir

½ ounce grenadine syrup (page 24)

Ready for your close-up? Pour the tequila over ice in a rocks glass and then add the orange juice. Slowly add the Pinot Noir by pouring it over the back of a spoon (rested against the glass's rim), allowing the liquid to sink to the bottom of the glass. Finish by slowly adding the grenadine.

SEX ON THE WATERFRONT

ON THE WATERFRONT (1954) DIRECTED BY ELIA KAZAN

On the Waterfront takes its name from the New Jersey docks on which former prizefighter Marlon Brando finds employment. When he witnesses an inside-job murder, Brando is compelled to confront the mixed-up morality of speaking out against his union boss—which compelled the Academy of Motion Picture Arts and Sciences to award Brando his first Oscar (of seven eventual nominations). Helmed by Elia Kazan, whose eye for previously untapped talent turned many an actor from unknown to A-lister, *Waterfront* was seen as a not-very-veiled rebuttal to the backlash the director received after naming names in the McCarthy trials. Our variation on a waterside classic uses "Smearnoff" campaign ingredients that'll have you on your knees—asking for another, if not for forgiveness.

1½ ounces vodka (like Smirnoff)

1 ounce pineapple juice

1 ounce cranberry juice

½ ounce orange juice

½ ounce crème de pêche liqueur

Combine all the ingredients with ice in a shaker and shake well. Strain over fresh ice in a Collins glass. Best drink ever? Could be a contender.

A SIDECAR NAMED DESIRE

Break out your tank tops! Based on Tennessee Williams's Pulitzer-winning play, *Streetcar* tells the steamy New Orleans story of one Blanche DuBois, a flighty, fading beauty whose unexpected arrival at her sister and brother-in-law's tiny apartment sets the stage for many a claustrophobic confrontation. This was the first film to win three Academy Awards in the acting categories, including one for Vivien Leigh, whose manic performance proved prescient for her own late-life diagnosis of bipolar disorder. When your own last-minute houseguests arrive, offer up this Southern sidecar, which will have them running into the streets shouting for seconds (and maybe a second chance).

2 ounces Southern Comfort

1 ounce lemon juice

¾ ounce Grand Marnier

Orange twist, for garnish

Set aside your beer (sorry: your Stelllllaaaaa!) and combine all the ingredients with ice in a shaker. Shake well, strain into a cocktail glass, and garnish with the orange twist.

CITIZEN GRAIN

CITIZEN KANE (1941) DIRECTED BY ORSON WELLES

A newspaper magnate's mysterious final utterance inspires a life told in flashback in what many critics hail as *the* best film of all time. (Take that, *Casablanca*, *Vertigo*, and *Showgirls*.) The titular Charles Foster Kane was so closely modeled on real-life news tycoon William Randolph Hearst that Hearst reportedly refused to see the film—or give it even an inch of ink in his own papers. A much-studied classic by any measure, *Kane* is doubly remarkable for being the first feature film from none other than Orson "War of the Worlds" Welles, who was only twenty-five at the time. (Doesn't that alone make you want to drink?) Toast to beginner's luck with a fizzy "rosebud" cocktail that'll let you have the last word.

2 ounces gin

½ ounce grain alcohol (like Everclear)

¾ ounce Lillet Blanc

¾ ounce simple syrup (page 25)

3 drops rose water

Sparkling water, to fill

3 blackberries, for garnish

Combine all the ingredients (except the sparkling water) with ice in a shaker and shake well. (*Note*: Don't overdo the grain alcohol, as it is extremely potent.) Strain over fresh ice in a highball glass and top with the sparkling water. Drop in a few blackberries for garnish. You'll be black and white and drunk all over.

BOURBON COWBOY

Picture *Saturday Night Fever* with mechanical bulls instead of disco balls, and you've got this oddball ode to working hard and drinking harder. A post-*Grease* (and still-hot) John Travolta stars as Bud, a Texas country bumpkin who moves to Houston to make a little money—and a lot of trouble. When Bud falls hard for honky-tonk regular and certifiable spitfire Sissy (Debra Winger, in a breakout performance), he ends up losing her over the sexist semantics of mechanical bull riding—which inspires Bud to ride the rump himself. Giddyup for our refined, big-city twist on a down-South classic.

4 basil leaves, divided

2 dashes Angostura bitters

2 ounces bourbon

1¼ ounces iced tea, sweetened to taste

½ ounce lemon juice

Muddle 3 basil leaves and the bitters in a shaker. Add the remaining ingredients and ice, and shake well. Strain into a julep cup (or a rocks glass) filled with freshly shaved ice and garnish with a basil leaf. Don't drink and ride.

BEN-HURRICANE

BEN-HUR (1959) DIRECTED BY WILLIAM WYLER

Hope your sofa's comfy! Clocking in at a little over three and a half hours, *Ben-Hur* is the tale of a fictional Jewish prince (Charlton "NRA" Heston) who, along with his family, is wrongly imprisoned and sent to the Roman galleys. After inspirational encounters with local celebrity Jesus Christ, Ben-Hur eventually gets his chance to exact revenge on the former friend who sent him to jail in the first place, culminating in the legendary chariot-racing scene that's still gripping today—not to mention brimming with homoerotic undertones. (Gore Vidal was one of the uncredited screenwriters.) Prepare to be a slave to our epic, passion-of-the-fruit cocktail that should help this movie speed by.

2 ounces light rum

2 ounces dark rum

2 ounces passion fruit juice

1 ounce orange juice

½ ounce lime juice

½ ounce lemon juice

½ ounce grenadine syrup (page 24)

Lemon wedge, for garnish

Lime wedge, for garnish

Orange wedge, for garnish

Cherry, for garnish

Move over, holy water—this drink is biblical. Pour the two rums into a Collins glass with ice. Add the remaining juices, pour the grenadine over top, and stir. Garnish with the fruits.

DO THE RYE THING

Picture a Brooklyn block right before the dawn of the planet of the hipsters, and you've got the setting for the damning (and damn smart) *Do the Right Thing*. Spanning a single, otherwise-ordinary day if not for the stifling heat, Lee's film cast a kaleidoscope of multigenerational talents as Bed-Stuy residents whose local pizzeria is at the center of boiling-over community commotion. Who else but a prodigy filmmaker could have pulled off this funny, furious film about race relations that ends on such a decidedly gray note? Grab a lawn chair, find some shade, and cool down your own hot head with a rye-whiskey refresher that stars corner-store staples.

3 ounces AriZona Iced Tea (Arnold Palmer
    Half & Half)
1 mini-bottle (or 1½ ounces) rye whiskey
Perrier, to fill
Lemon-lime Popsicle

Get your boom box out of storage and your mix tapes out of the closet. Now, pour the tea into a mason jar and add the whiskey. Add the Perrier to fill, and stir with the Popsicle to chill and flavor.

RAGING RED BULL

RAGING BULL (1980) DIRECTED BY MARTIN SCORSESE

Dream team Robert De Niro and Martin Scorsese put their heads together after the actor read bruiser Jake LaMotta's autobiography and thought it would be a perfect fit for his *Taxi Driver* director. No fan of boxing, Scorsese initially balked, but several years (and writers) later, the duo got back in the ring for what would become one of the eighties' most talked-about films. Told in flashback after an opening sequence that had De Niro gaining a hefty sixty pounds, *Raging Bull* is an unflinching look at how a man's greatest strength at work can also be his greatest weakness at home. Our own heart-pounding, Italian-American thirst-quencher will have you going one more round.

1 ounce Campari
1 ounce sweet vermouth
1 ounce gin
½ ounce Red Bull

Place all the ingredients in a mixing glass with ice and stir well. Strain into a rocks glass over fresh ice and prepare to see stars.

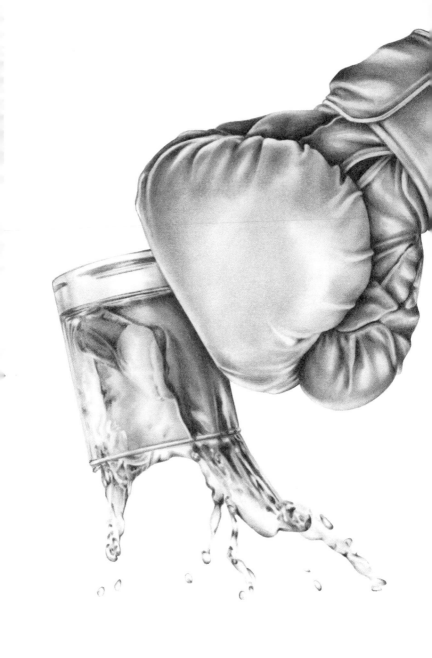

GONE WITH THE GIN

GONE WITH THE WIND (1939) DIRECTED BY VICTOR FLEMING

In the days before televised talent contests, this film's forward-thinking producer launched a national search for his leading lady, landing on the very British Vivien Leigh to play the very Southern Scarlett O'Hara—bossy belle of the high-and-mightiest order. Leigh's feisty on-screen chemistry with Clark Gable remains both immortal and also a tad misleading. They famously challenged each other on-set, which may have helped shoot the Civil War–themed *Wind* into the history books as a top-earning, unrelenting, riches-to-rags melodrama. Our hot-as-a-burning-Atlanta hooch is sure to start a few of your own battles—at least over who gets the first pour.

2 whole jalapeños, halved and seeded

½ peach, pitted and sliced

2 rosemary sprigs, divided

¾ ounce simple syrup (page 25)

1½ ounces gin

½ ounce Campari

½ ounce lemon juice

Club soda, to fill

Muddle the jalapeños, peach, 1 rosemary sprig, and simple syrup in a shaker. Add the gin, Campari, lemon juice, and a handful of ice to the shaker and shake well. Double-strain over fresh ice in a rocks glass, fill with the club soda, and garnish with the remaining rosemary sprig. Sip slow—you've got three-plus hours to get through.

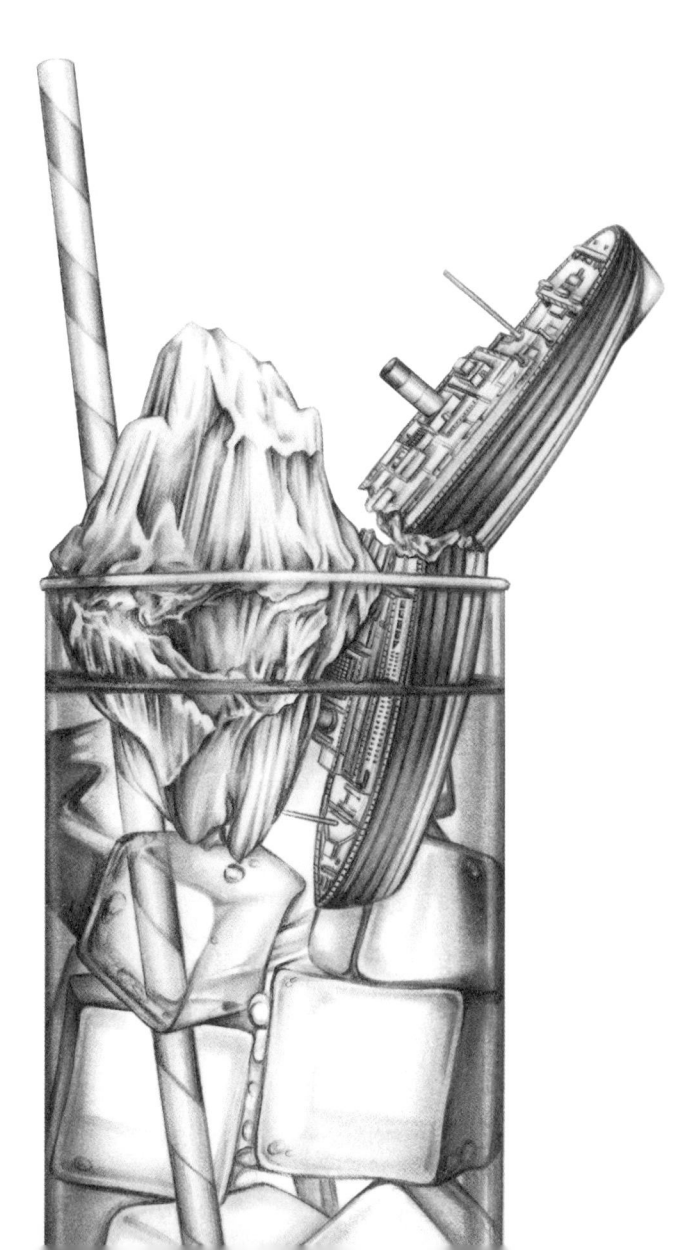

TI-TONIC

TITANIC (1997) DIRECTED BY JAMES CAMERON

One of the twentieth century's biggest disasters also inspired its biggest box-office hit. With so much hype surrounding James Cameron's mega-moneymaker—there was a two-year span during which you couldn't turn on a radio without hearing Celine Dion's heart go on—it's notable to recall that *Titanic* actually tied with *Ben-Hur* for the most Oscar nominations in history. This Romeo-and-Juliet-on-the-high-seas romance inspires a tragically good drink. You'll be the king of the bar, if not the world.

2 ounces mezcal

$1\frac{1}{2}$ tablespoons honey

$\frac{1}{2}$ ounce Aperol

3 drops salt water (mix $\frac{1}{2}$ teaspoon salt into
   $\frac{1}{4}$ cup warm water)

4 ounces tonic water

Combine the mezcal, honey, and Aperol with ice in a shaker and shake well. In lieu of an actual iceberg, strain over ice in a Collins glass and add the salt water. Top with the tonic water.

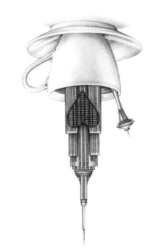

COMEDIES

> "If anyone orders Merlot, I'm leaving.
> I am *not* drinking any fucking Merlot!"
>
> —Paul Giamatti (as Miles) in *Sideways*

Welcome to the section that contains more happy endings than a back-alley massage parlor. From the Coen brothers to the Ephron sisters, whether sly satire or raucous rom-com, each of these funny-boned films had audiences rolling in the aisles—and their corresponding cocktails will have you giggling in the kitchen. Pay tribute to one of Hollywood's oldest and most enduring genres, the can't-get-no-respect comedies that win laughs instead of Oscars. Slap your knees and smack your lips!

YOU'VE GOT ALE

YOU'VE GOT MAIL (1998) DIRECTED BY NORA EPHRON

If you've ever fallen in love with someone on the Internet only to meet the "real them" in person, you'll understand the timeless appeal of *You've Got Mail*, an AOL-era twist on the oft-adapted "shop around the corner" premise. Then-bankable box office pair Meg Ryan and Tom Hanks play opposite each other as bitter rivals in the David-versus-Goliath world of bookselling, neither of them realizing that they're already acquainted thanks to anonymous flirtations. Re-"kindle" your love of books (if not online dating) with this perfectly paired bubbles-meets-brawn beverage.

4 ounces ale

2 ounces ginger ale

2 ounces Champagne

Pour the ale into a pint glass, add the ginger ale, and top with the Champagne. Swipe right on this one, and hope it's a match!

SOME SPIKE IT HOT

SOME LIKE IT HOT (1959) DIRECTED BY BILLY WILDER

Often cited as the greatest comedy of all time, *Some Like It Hot* put Jack Lemmon and Tony Curtis into dresses—and sent audiences into stitches. In a playful plot, two Chicagoland musicians go unconventionally undercover after accidentally witnessing the real-life St. Valentine's Day Massacre. The film also stars Marilyn Monroe as history's most unlikely ukulele player. Toast to this madcap masterpiece with a hot hooch that'll have you seeing, well, *cross*-eyed.

1 teaspoon brown sugar

1 tablespoon unsalted butter

6 ounces hot tap water

2 ounces dark rum

Pinch of ground nutmeg

Lemon zest, for garnish

Microwave the brown sugar and butter for 15 seconds in a mug. Swirl the butter inside the mug and then discard the liquid. Add the water and rum, and garnish with the nutmeg and lemon zest on top. And remember: No wigs, no heels, no service.

WHISKEY BUSINESS

RISKY BUSINESS (1983) DIRECTED BY PAUL BRICKMAN

Gentlemen, oil your floors. Easy to dismiss as a "craziest weekend ever" teen comedy, *Risky Business* actually had seriously satirical things to say about the ultra-excess of eighties capitalism, from Porsches to Princeton. (It also had a young Tom Cruise boogying around in his underwear, so there's that.) Take note, suburban readers: This film skewers the culture of upper-middle-class parents whose crushing expectations can turn any kid from a baby-faced suburbanite to a brothel-dwelling entrepreneur. Break into your dad's best whiskey for an up-all-night beverage that'll be worth the risk.

> 1 ounce good whiskey (like Glenmorangie)
> ¾ ounce sherry
> ½ ounce Bénédictine

Combine all the ingredients over ice in a mixing glass and stir well. Strain into a rocks glass, pop your collar, and get drinking—and dancing.

THE MUPPETS MAKE MANHATTANS

THE MUPPETS TAKE MANHATTAN (1984) DIRECTED BY FRANK OZ

Everyone's favorite marionettes-slash-puppets return for their take on the old Mickey-and-Judy "Let's put on a show!" trope. Here, Kermit & Co. celebrate graduating from college with a show-tune revue that gets such great buzz, they decide to take the show to Broadway—despite their fretful frog leader's misgivings. Shot on location in New York and with everyone from Liza Minnelli to Joan Rivers making cameos, this film also introduced the Muppet Babies in a dream sequence that proved such a hit, they got their own Saturday morning spin-off cartoon. Whether bound for the big time or not, you'll be sent off with a song once you get a taste of this Big Apple Manhattan.

2 ounces apple brandy

¾ ounce sweet vermouth

½ ounce apple juice

1½ teaspoons honey

3 dashes baked apple bitters

Green apple slice, for garnish

Combine all the ingredients (except for the green apple slice) with ice in a mixing glass and stir well. Strain into a cocktail glass, garnish with the apple—and serve with a side of bacon (with apologies to Miss Piggy).

LUSHMORE

RUSHMORE (1998) DIRECTED BY WES ANDERSON

Though he'd scored critical cheers with his first film *Bottle Rocket*, it wasn't until *Rushmore* that Wes Anderson gained the attention of the relative masses—at least in indie-film terms. With *Harold and Maude*–like themes of an overscheduled prep school sophomore (Jason Schwartzman), whose adoration of a young widow (Olivia Williams) puts him at odds with a love-struck millionaire (Bill Murray's comeback role), *Rushmore* was shot on a shoestring budget with style to spare. Get schooled with our precocious take on a kid-worthy, chocolate-milk classic.

4 ounces chocolate milk

1 ounce bourbon

½ ounce crème de cacao liqueur

½ ounce simple syrup (page 25)

3 mini marshmallows, for garnish

Combine all the ingredients (except for the marshmallows) in a shaker and dry shake. Pour over ice in a highball glass and top with the marshmallows. This one ought to score some extra credit.

MRS. STOUT-FIRE

MRS. DOUBTFIRE (1993) DIRECTED BY CHRIS COLUMBUS

In the film's titular role, Robin Williams plays an actor who specializes in cartoon voiceovers, showcasing all the high-energy hilarity that made him one of Hollywood's most beloved stars. It didn't hurt to have him playing opposite America's sweetheart Sally Field as his divorced wife looking for help around the house (enter: Williams in a wig), even if critics largely derided the film as a sappy slog. Try a drink that's anything but a drag when you dress up stout with a Scottish liqueur accent. Just watch for lipstick on the rim.

> 1 ounce ginger liqueur
> ¾ ounce honey liqueur (like Drambuie)
> 3 ounces milk stout beer
> Pinch of cayenne pepper

Pour the liqueurs over ice in a highball glass and top with the beer. Stir well and add the cayenne pepper. Serve with a side of, uh, sausage?

THE 7 & 7 YEAR ITCH

THE SEVEN YEAR ITCH (1955) DIRECTED BY BILLY WILDER

In *The Seven Year Itch*, a straightlaced publishing exec's wife and kid hightail it out of Manhattan for the summer, leaving Dad alone just as a hotshot new neighbor (hello, Marilyn Monroe!) moves in. Despite its saucy setup, this film was shot during the puritanical height of Hollywood's censors, leading even its own director to later denounce it as too chaste to elicit many thrills. With a title derived from the term that suggests a marriage starts to lose its steam after seven years, this film inspires a cool summer soda that goes best in a copper mug—the traditional seventh-anniversary gift, of course.

> 2 ounces whiskey (like Seagram's)
>
> 3 ounces lemon-lime soda
>
> 3 ounces ginger beer

Pour the whiskey over ice in a copper mug (or a rocks glass), and add the soda and ginger beer. You'll be standing over subway grates in no time.

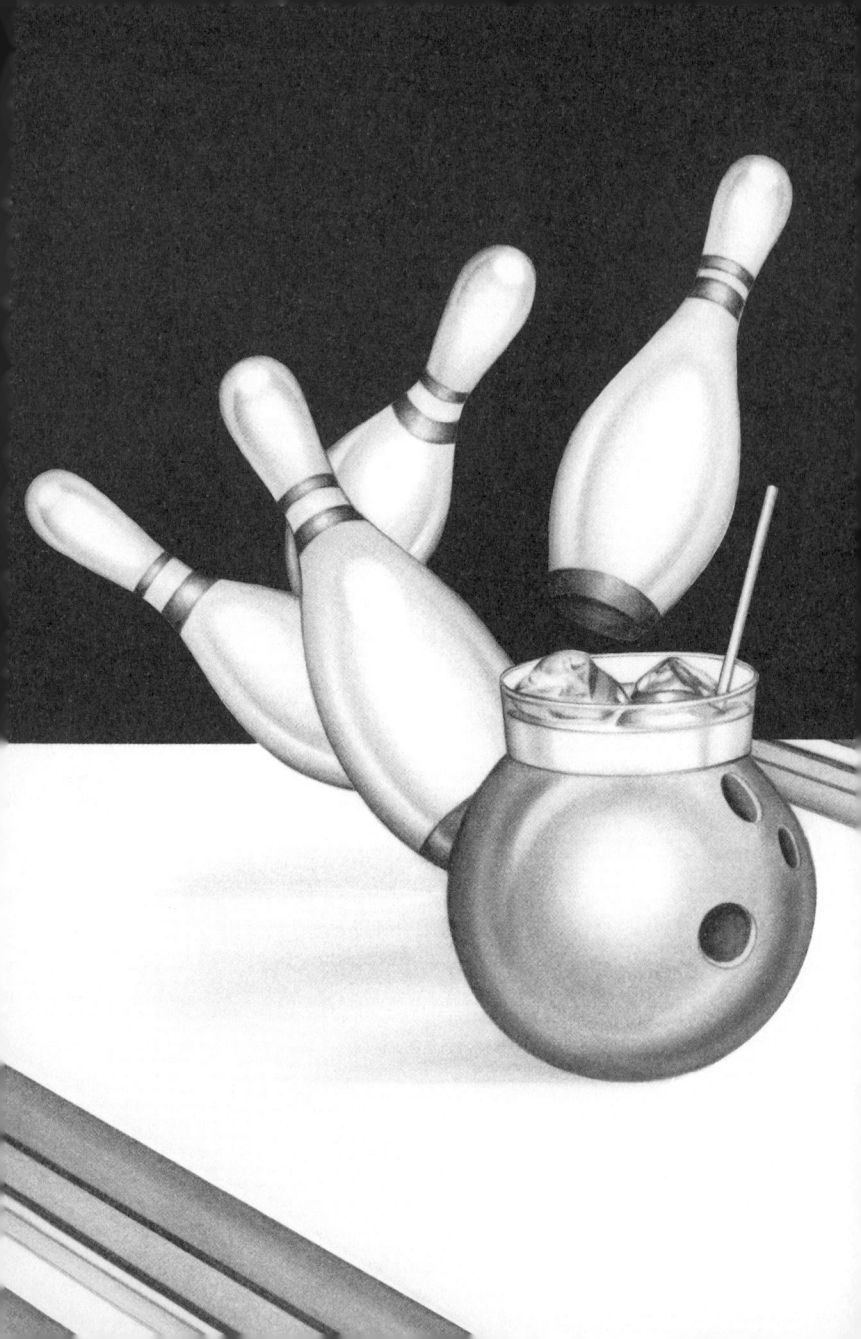

THE BIG LE-BREWSKI

THE BIG LEBOWSKI (1998) DIRECTED BY THE COEN BROTHERS

This trippy crime caper finds a Southern-Cali slacker named Jeffrey Lebowski chasing down an elusive millionaire—also named Jeffrey Lebowski—after the first Jeffrey suffers a mistaken identity mixup that launches him on a hilariously convoluted journey. Featuring more pornographic subplots than you can shake a bowling pin at and enough f-bombs to make a sailor blush, *Lebowski* may have been a dud when it debuted, but it has since achieved cult status as a midnight-movie staple. You'll be The Dude when you make your buddies our fresh-brewed twist on the sometimes-underestimated White Russian.

2 ounces vodka

2 ounces cold-brew coffee

2 ounces cream of coconut

Talk about a dream sequence: Pour the vodka over ice in a rocks glass, add the coffee, top with the cream of coconut, and stir.

MONTY PYTHON
AND THE STOLI GRAIL

MONTY PYTHON AND THE HOLY GRAIL (1975)
DIRECTED BY TERRY GILLIAM AND TERRY JONES

Killer bunnies, knights who say "Ni," and God himself are just a smattering of the zany supporting characters who appear in this legendary cult satire from Britain's madcap Monty Python comedy troupe. Chronicling the quest of King Arthur & Co. on their bloody hilarious (and just plain bloody) search for the Holy Grail, the film was shot on such a tight budget that they couldn't even afford horses, leading to an infamous bit in which a footman claps together two coconut shells to simulate "hooves." Your own search for the perfect drink will come to a conclusion with our coconutty cocktail.

$1\frac{1}{2}$ ounces vodka (like Stoli)

1 ounce light rum

1 ounce coconut water

$\frac{3}{4}$ ounce pineapple juice

Combine all the ingredients with ice in a shaker and shake well. Strain over fresh ice in a rocks glass—or a grail, if one has finally been discovered.

SLOPPY IN SEATTLE

SLEEPLESS IN SEATTLE (1993) DIRECTED BY NORA EPHRON

The rare romantic comedy in which the leads don't even meet till the final scene, *Sleepless* cast the nineties' most dateable duo as its lonely, long-distance lovers. Tom Hanks is the recently widowered Washington-state architect whose son wants Dad to find love again. Meg Ryan is the Maryland reporter who hears the father-son saga on a call-in radio show. And the Empire State Building is the *Affair to Remember*–evoking meeting place that finally brings the two together—which, in turn, brought audiences in by the weeping busload. You'll be up all night after our Seattle-worthy coffee cocktail that's worth staying awake for.

Shot of espresso
1 ounce whiskey
½ ounce amaro liqueur
Ground cinnamon, for garnish

Brew the espresso and pour into a small mug. Add the whiskey and amaro, and sprinkle the cinnamon on top. Serve warm—and get out the Kleenex!

THRILLERS

> "A census taker once tried to test me.
> I ate his liver with some fava beans
> and a nice Chianti."
>
> —Anthony Hopkins (as Hannibal Lecter) in
> *The Silence of the Lambs*

Lock the doors. Draw the blinds. Grab a glass! The following classics contain enough surprise twists to make M. Night Shyamalan jealous— and that's just the drinks. If your idea of a feel-good film involves a double-digit body count, this is the section for you. From Hitchcock hounds to Scorsese supporters, whether you're a gun moll, gangster, burglar, or boogeyman, fasten your seatbelts for the bumpiest beverages in the whole book. You'll be shaking (and straining) in your boots.

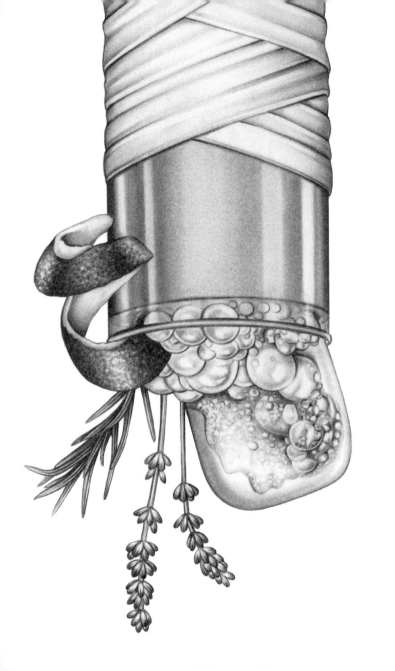

FIGHT CLUB SODA

FIGHT CLUB (1999) DIRECTED BY DAVID FINCHER

The first rule of Fight Club Soda is you do not *hiccup* talk about Fight Club Soda! Featuring Brad Pitt as the least-likely soap maker ever, alongside a very fit Edward Norton as a very *un*fit office worker, David Fincher's coming-of-rage manifesto on materialism divided critics as one of the most brutally violent movies of the last millennium. Seems appropriate, then, that a film featuring an underground society would become a massive cult success, itself; DVD sales went through the roof, establishing *Fight Club* as a like-it-or-not movie mainstay. For such a potent picture, our soap-scented soda may smell sweet—but it pulls no punches.

2 ounces gin

1 ounce Lillet Blanc

$\frac{1}{2}$ ounce grapefruit juice

3 dashes lavender bitters

3 ounces club soda

$\frac{1}{2}$ ounce crème de violette liqueur

Lavender sprig, for garnish

Grapefruit twist, for garnish

Movie night with the fellas? Pour the gin, Lillet Blanc, grapefruit juice, and bitters over ice in a highball glass, add the club soda, and slowly pour the crème de violette on top. Garnish with the sprig of lavender and grapefruit twist—and head to the basement.

NO COUNTRY FOR OLD FASHIONEDS

Call the sheriff the next time you stumble upon two million bucks, lest you find yourself chased by a money-hungry hit man who flips coins to decide who lives. Such is the premise behind the Coen brothers' mega-violent but gorgeously shot film—packed with hotel hideouts, laconic lawmen, and truly questionable haircuts. A slow-starter at the box office, these old men eventually ran off with Oscar gold, nabbing four top awards in a year that counted *There Will Be Blood* among its cold-hearted contenders. Our smoky Tex-Mex take on an old standby is finished off with a bitter(s) bite that'll have you begging—for another.

> 2 ounces mezcal
> Dash of agave nectar
> 2 drops chocolate mole bitters
> Grapefruit twist, for garnish

Pour the mezcal, agave, and bitters into a mixing glass. Fill with ice and stir well. Strain into a rocks glass over fresh ice, garnish with the grapefruit twist—and run for your life.

THE FRENCH CONCOCTION

Based on a real-life, late-sixties case in which two New York City police officers brought down an immense overseas heroin ring, this movie—the first R-rated flick to win Best Pic at the Oscars—was shot so fast, loose, and dirty, portions of it practically play out like a documentary. Famously, *French* featured a porkpie-wearing Gene Hackman in what many consider to be the craftiest (and subsequently most-imitated) car chase ever caught on pre-Steadicam film. Calm your jitters with a Marseilles twist on a throwback concoction that was first smuggled into the states from Harry's New York Bar—in France.

> 1½ ounces gin
> ½ ounce lemon juice
> ½ ounce pastis
> 3 ounces Champagne
> Lemon twist, for garnish

Combine the gin, lemon juice, and pastis in a shaker with ice. Shake well, strain into a flute, and top with Champagne. Garnish with the lemon twist—and find out how to say "delicious" in French.

DIRTY HARRY MARTINI

DIRTY HARRY (1971) DIRECTED BY DON SIEGEL

I've got to ask you one question: "Do you feel lucky?" Well, do ya—*drunk*?! Though pretty much every star from Frank Sinatra to Paul Newman to John Wayne was offered a chance to do Harry's dirty deeds, Clint Eastwood eventually landed the role as the Bay Area, .44 Magnum–wielding vigilante copper. Inspired by the real-life Zodiac serial killer case (turned into its own nail-biter of a film in 2007), *Harry* proved popular enough to launch four additional movies. Our extra-dirty martini will likely inspire your own repeat visits—at least to the bar.

3 ounces gin
¾ ounce pickle juice
¼ ounce dry vermouth

If Eastwood can do all his own stunts, you can make your own martini. Combine all the ingredients with ice in a shaker and shake well. Double-strain into a cocktail glass.

65¢ 1ST ⅙ MILE

TAXI SCREW-DRIVER

TAXI DRIVER (1976) DIRECTED BY MARTIN SCORSESE

Buckle up for a frightening film that won innumerable accolades (though, curiously, no Oscars) and permanently placed De Niro and Scorsese at the top of the list of Hollywood's toughest talents. Tracing the downward spiral of Travis Bickle, whose career behind the wheel is a far cry from his days in Vietnam, *Taxi Driver* also brought a thirteen-year-old Jodie Foster to prominence. Not to be out-acted by his middle-school costar, De Niro was so "method," he reportedly got his cab license in his spare time—when he wasn't improvising one of the most quoted pieces of dialogue ever—"You talkin' to me?" This rough ride inspires a blood(y)-orange take on a classic cocktail.

> 1 ounce vodka
> 1 ounce gin
> 6 ounces blood orange juice
> Blood orange wedge, for garnish

Hide your car keys, pour the vodka and gin over ice in a highball glass, and top with the blood orange juice. Give it a quick stir and garnish with the wedge of blood orange.

BONNIE AND MUDSLIDE

Based on a pair of real-life bank robbers, *Bonnie and Clyde* brought a taste for bloodbaths (and a surge in beret sales) to mainstream masses, in spite of a squeamish studio that initially tried burying its own film. Though critics were divided over the movie's unprecedented gore and guts, audiences came out in droves to see Faye Dunaway and Warren Beatty shoot 'em up in style. Our Mudslide mash-up proves that two indelible ingredients are even more dangerous when combined.

2 ounces vodka

2 ounces Kahlúa

1 ounce whole milk

Espresso bean, for garnish

Pour the vodka and Kahlúa over ice in a rocks glass. Slowly add the milk and stir to combine ingredients. Float an espresso bean on top to finish with a bang!

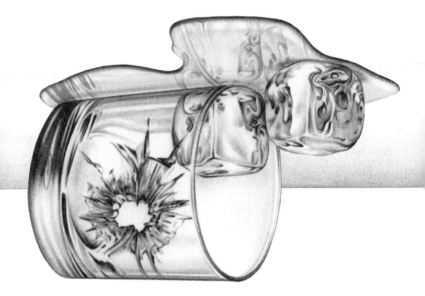

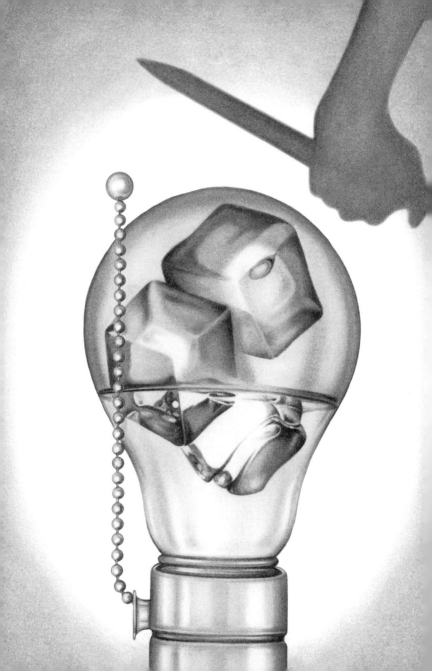

WAIT UNTIL DARK
AND STORMY

WAIT UNTIL DARK (1967) DIRECTED BY TERENCE YOUNG

Adapted from a smash Broadway play, *Wait Until Dark* remains creepy (if slightly creaky) fun even today. The film stars Audrey Hepburn as a recently blind, recently wed downtown dame, whose husband is just trying to do a stranger a favor when he provides safe harbor for her baby doll—which, by the way, ends up being stuffed with heroin. (Hey, we've all been there.) When a gang of goons tracks the doll down to Hepburn's home, she outsmarts them in a fiery showdown that left audiences in the dark (legend has it theater-owners across America even switched off the overheads to heighten the impact). Get lit with our take on a quintessential cocktail that's so simple, you could make it with your eyes shut.

2 ounces spiced rum or dark rum (whichever
  you grab in the dark)
½ ounce lemon (or lime) juice
Ginger beer (or ginger ale), to fill

Pour the rum and lemon juice over ice in a highball glass and fill to the top with the ginger beer. Now hit the lights and get down to business.

THE MOON-SHINING

In this controversial Kubrick picture, an alcoholic writer and his young family head to the Overlook Hotel to take up winter residence as its lone caretakers—or so they think. This being a loosey-goosey adaptation of a novel by Stephen King (an outspoken foe of the film), the mountainside resort complex brims with ghostly life, not to mention death. Viewers expecting a fast-paced fright fest instead get a hypnotically eerie maze of a movie, which some consider the most enthralling thriller of all time—despite it receiving zero Oscar nominations. Next time you're snowed in with only a few supplies on hand, you'll say "Cheeeeers, Johnny!" for our red-rum moonshine masterpiece.

1 ounce ruby red grapefruit juice

1 ounce light rum

½ ounce "moonshine" (like Midnight Moon)

Put down the axe and pour all the ingredients over ice—or snow—in a rocks glass. Give it a quick stir.

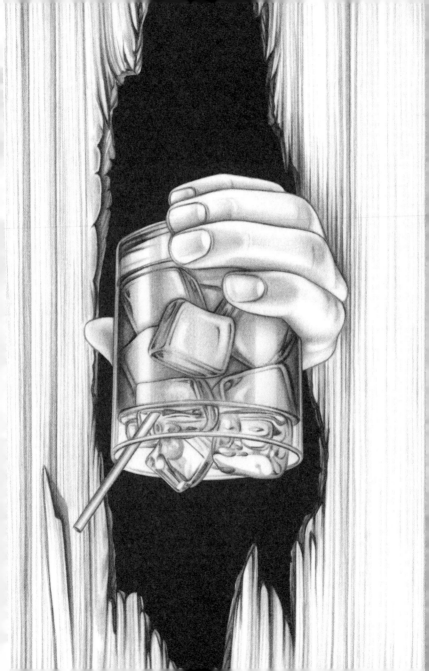

THE MARASCHINO CANDIDATE

THE MANCHURIAN CANDIDATE (1962) DIRECTED BY JOHN FRANKENHEIMER

A Cold War–era hit big enough to inspire a modern remake (starring Denzel Washington and Meryl Streep), the original *Candidate* concerns a Korean War hero (and Medal of Honor recipient) who becomes unwittingly entangled in a presidential assassination. Not only groundbreaking as the first film to cast black actors in roles for which race was never specified, *Manchurian* also has Angela Lansbury smooching her son in a performance so cunning, she had to head to Broadway for a few years before anyone in Hollywood would consider her for less sinister roles. With a wink to costar Frank Sinatra's famous eyes, one sip of our blue brainwasher and you'll be ensnared in cherry-picked plots you never saw coming.

> 1 ounce gin
> 1 ounce lime juice
> 1 ounce maraschino cherry liqueur (like Luxardo)
> ½ ounce simple syrup (page 25)
> ½ ounce blue curaçao
> Maraschino cherry, for garnish

Combine all the liquid ingredients with ice in a shaker. Shake well, strain into a highball glass over fresh ice, and top with the maraschino cherry. Talk about hypnotizing!

REAR WINO

Imagine being stuck indoors for over a month. In a heat wave. In a wheelchair. Without WiFi! And now you've got the setup to what's often hailed as one of Hitchcock's finest (and friskiest) films. James Stewart is the handsome invalid here, passing the weeks by spying on a colorful cross section of courtyard neighbors—till one of them begins acting a bit suspicious, and our hero's voyeurism threatens to turn him into the next murder victim. (Thank goodness Grace Kelly helps save the day, in style.) Next time *you're* housebound in the summer, stir up some suspense the old-fashioned way: by cracking open a window and slamming down our white-wine spritzer.

>   4 ounces white wine
>   2 ounces Prosecco
>   1 ounce elderflower liqueur

Pour all the ingredients over ice in a wine glass and give it a swirl. You'll *definitely* be seeing things.

MUSICALS

> "Rum punch. Quite satisfactory.
> *hiccup*"
>
> —Julie Andrews (as Mary Poppins) in *Mary Poppins*

There are two kinds of people: those who break into song in the middle of the sidewalk and those who, well, don't. OK, So maybe a bunch of blonde pretty-boys pirouetting in the alleys of Manhattan isn't your idea of a "gang." Maybe you secretly wish the Wicked Witch *had* turned the Scarecrow into kindling. Whatever your tastes, don't rule out the mighty, merry movie musical just yet. Some of this book's loudest libations can be found in this section. You might just sing, yet.

THE ROCKY HORROR PISCO SHOW

THE ROCKY HORROR PICTURE SHOW (1975) DIRECTED BY JIM SHARMAN

You can still catch a midnight screening of this sordid songfest nearly a half-century after its lukewarm debut, which was adapted from a London stage production that featured a soon-to-be-infamous cross-dresser played by Tim Curry. A don't-squint-too-hard-at-the-details plot concerns young-in-love Susan Sarandon and Barry Bostwick pulling into the wrong driveway at the right time, becoming exposed (in every sense of the word) to a madcap cast of punk rockers and blonde beefcakes. One sip of our red-as-lips libation, and you'll be shouting at the screen—whether you know the legendary lyrics or not.

2 ounces pisco brandy

1 ounce cranberry juice

¾ ounce lime juice

½ ounce Cointreau

Combine all the ingredients with ice in a mixing glass and strain into a cocktail glass. Serve with an extra helping of Meat Loaf.

YANKEE DOODLE BRANDY

YANKEE DOODLE DANDY (1942) DIRECTED BY MICHAEL CURTIZ

George M. Cohan provided much of the soundtrack for the early twentieth century, including "You're a Grand Old Flag" and this film's title tune. His incredible life—from a childhood performing in vaudeville, all the way to the White House (where he received a Congressional Gold Medal from FDR)—plays here like a musicalized, I-can't-believe-how-many-things-one-guy-could-accomplish version of *Forrest Gump.* In the role of Cohan, Oscar-winner Jimmy Cagney can't really sing or dance—but then, is anything more American than faking it till you make it? Be a patriot with an American-as-apple-brandy beverage that'll have you saluting more than flags.

Green apple slice

2 brandied cherries (page 23), divided

1 teaspoon maple syrup

2 dashes Angostura bitters

2 ounces American apple brandy

Place the apple slice and one cherry at the bottom of a rocks glass. Add the maple syrup and bitters, and muddle the ingredients. Fill the glass with ice, add the brandy, and garnish with the other cherry—skewering it with an American-flag toothpick, of course.

BOOZY AND THE BEAST

BEAUTY AND THE BEAST (1991) DIRECTED BY GARY TROUSDALE AND KIRK WISE

The first animated film ever nominated for Best Picture at the Academy Awards, this beauty proved cartoons don't just belong to Saturday mornings—or to kids, for that matter. One of the crown jewels of Disney's decade-long animation renaissance (a hit-after-hit slate that included belting mermaids and wisecracking genies), *Beast* populated its castle with feisty feather dusters, crabby clocks, and a tuneful teapot (as portrayed by Angela Lansbury, who legendarily nailed Alan Menken and Howard Ashman's title song in one tear-inducing take). Be our guest and have a spot of tipsy tea topped with a petal.

Hibiscus tea (bag or loose)

1 teaspoon shredded coconut

1½ ounces light rum

1 ounce coconut water

¾ ounce simple syrup (page 25)

½ ounce lemon juice

Hibiscus petal, for garnish

Steep the tea and coconut in a teapot for 10 minutes, strain approximately 3 ounces into a teacup, and set aside. Pour the rum, coconut water, simple syrup, and lemon juice into a shaker, and dry shake. Add to the teacup and garnish with the hibiscus petal. Just make sure to drink it before time runs out—or the water runs cold.

ALL THAT FIZZ

ALL THAT JAZZ (1979) DIRECTED BY BOB FOSSE

In the early seventies there were few people as prolific as director-choreographer Bob Fosse, who won an Emmy, an Oscar, and a Tony—all in the same year. Fueling such an aggressive career were equal parts pills, booze, and cigarettes—lots of cigarettes—in addition to a handful of wives and a whole bunch of showgirls. This on-the-edge lifestyle was chronicled in Fosse's semiautobiographical *All That Jazz*, a razzmatazz musical tragicomedy that featured Roy "You're gonna need a bigger boat" Scheider as Fosse's doppelgänger, with a young Jessica Lange appearing as his Angel of Death. Celebrate a complicated genius with our heavenly white fizz, whose smoky finish is heart-stoppingly delicious.

¼ ounce single malt scotch

1 egg white

2 ounces gin

1 ounce lemon juice

¾ ounce simple syrup (page 25)

2 dashes orange blossom water

2 ounces club soda

It's showtime! Coat the inside of a cocktail glass with the scotch, dispose of the liquid, and set the glass aside. Add all the remaining ingredients (except the club soda) to the shaker and dry shake for 10 seconds. Add a handful of ice to the shaker and shake for an additional few seconds. Strain into the cocktail glass and top with the club soda.

BLOODY MARY POPPINS

MARY POPPINS (1964) DIRECTED BY ROBERT STEVENSON

Mary Poppins took a turbulent flight on her way to the big screen, beginning with Walt Disney's fifteen-year quest to secure the film rights from Australian novelist P. L. Travers. Their cat-and-Mickey-Mouse negotiations paid off, and audiences came out in record numbers to see Julie Andrews in her cinematic, Oscar-sweeping debut. Your turn to work some magic: Try saying "Supercalifragilisticexpialidocious" after tipsily toasting the original tough-love nanny. Our bloody-good, British-gin twist on a legendary libation doesn't even require a spoonful of sugar.

4 ounces tomato juice

2 ounces dry London gin

1 tablespoon fresh grated ginger

1 teaspoon celery salt

1 teaspoon apple cider vinegar

1 teaspoon black pepper

1 teaspoon cayenne pepper

3 dashes Worcestershire sauce

Combine all the ingredients in a mixing glass and stir well. Pour the whole thing over ice in a Collins glass. Get ready to float on air.

THE WIZARD OF SHIRAZ

THE WIZARD OF OZ (1939) DIRECTED BY VICTOR FLEMING

This wonderful *Wizard* actually stumbled down a rocky brick road on its path to family-film infamy: Margaret Hamilton endured third-degree burns shooting the scene in which the Wicked Witch disappears in a cloud of (actual) smoke; the original Tin Man had to quit when the aluminum makeup began suffocating him through his skin (if I only had a *dermatologist*); and "Over the Rainbow" was nearly scrapped by MGM, who was nervous the ballad would go over the little heads of its audience. (Good thing the Oscar-winning tune stayed.) These days, we're staying in to stream our movies, so heat up some mulled wine to help make any house smell like home.

5 ounces Shiraz

1 ounce cognac

1 tablespoon honey

1 teaspoon allspice

1 teaspoon cardamom

1 teaspoon orange zest

Combine all the ingredients in a saucepan and bring to a boil. Reduce the heat and let simmer for 15 minutes. Remove from the stove, click your heels three times, and strain into a mug.

WHITE RUSSIAN CHRISTMAS

WHITE CHRISTMAS (1954) DIRECTED BY MICHAEL CURTIZ

A 1954 box-office gift that keeps on giving, this festive film features the catchiest Christmas songs ever written by nice Jewish boy Irving Berlin. In *White Christmas*, two World-War-II-soldiers-turned-song-and-dance-men discover a sister act with whom they team up to help revive an old Vermont inn—that just so happens to be run by the gents' former general. The movie features dazzling dancing and the formidable vocal chops of one Rosemary Clooney (George's aunt), opposite lead crooner Bing Crosby—who actually debuted the title song more than a decade earlier on his own radio show. Get in the holiday spirit(s) with a White Russian eggnog that's sure to make your days minty and bright.

> $1\frac{1}{2}$ ounces vodka
>
> 1 ounce crème de menthe liqueur
>
> 1 ounce Irish coffee liqueur (like Baileys)
>
> $\frac{1}{4}$ ounce eggnog
>
> Crushed candy cane, for garnish

Pour the vodka and crème de menthe over ice in a rocks glass. Combine the coffee liqueur and eggnog in a separate cup and, after untangling the Christmas tree lights, slowly add the eggnog mix to the rocks glass. Garnish with crushed candy cane pieces.

WEST CIDER STORY

Warm up your jazz hands, 'cause Romeo and Juliet are heading to the big city. Sure, it's hard not to giggle at the sight of teen gangs pirouetting toward each other in the mean streets—even if most of the teens were pushing thirty and half the mean streets were shot on Hollywood back lots—but *West Side*'s soaring score remains certifiably goose bump–inducing. Orbiting around the star-crossed romance of teenagers Tony and Maria, the film's themes of interracial romance and youth violence still echo note-for-note-true today. Our unlikely blend of New York–state apples and Puerto Rican rum is a fortified face-off that'll have you setting down switchblades and picking up glasses.

> 2 ounces Caribbean rum (like Bacardi 8)
> 1 ounce pineapple juice
> ½ ounce falernum
> 4 mint sprigs
> 3 ounces sparkling apple cider

Combine the rum, pineapple juice, falernum, and mint with ice in a shaker and shake well. Strain over fresh ice in a highball glass, top with sparkling cider, and go sing a love song on the fire escape.

LITTLE SCHNAPPS
OF HORRORS

LITTLE SHOP OF HORRORS (1986) DIRECTED BY FRANK OZ

Directed by the prolific puppeteer behind Miss Piggy and Yoda, this humorous *Horrors* show was adapted from an off-Broadway hit that was itself based on a 1960 B-movie version featuring a young Jack Nicholson. Set on an all-American skid row (but filmed on a British soundstage), the musical starred Rick Moranis as sad-sack Seymour, whose discovery of a rare plant helps turn a struggling neighborhood flower shop around—till said plant begins eating the neighbors, that is. You'll give two green thumbs up to this all-plant-based cocktail with a verdant Red Vine finish.

1½ ounces tequila

¾ ounce elderflower liqueur

½ ounce Green Chartreuse liqueur

¼ ounce Galliano liqueur

¼ ounce melon schnapps

Red Vine candy straw, for garnish

Pour all the ingredients (except for the Red Vine) into a mixing glass, add ice, and stir well. Strain into a cocktail glass and garnish with a Red Vine candy "straw." (No humans were harmed in the making of this drink.)

SIPPIN' IN THE RAIN

SINGIN' IN THE RAIN (1952) DIRECTED BY STANLEY DONEN AND GENE KELLY

In *Singin' in the Rain*, silent film stuntman and former hoofer Don Lockwood (Gene Kelly, also the film's co-director) is happy to make the literal leap into speaking roles—if only the voice of his famed on-screen romantic partner, Lina Lamont, didn't sound like nails on a chalkboard. Lucky for Lockwood, his chorus girl crush (a twenty-year-old Debbie Reynolds) has a voice sent from heaven above. Naturally, she steps in to speak up for Lamont, comedic chaos ensues, and boy gets girl (and gets wet) in the end. One of the most iconic dance sequences ever captured on film inspires this all-weather get-up-and-go drink that's guaranteed to send you skipping down sidewalks.

4 ounces Champagne

1½ ounces orange juice

¾ ounce raspberry liqueur

Raspberry, for garnish

Ready to make a splash? Pour all the ingredients into a flute, drop in the raspberry, and garnish with a mini-umbrella.

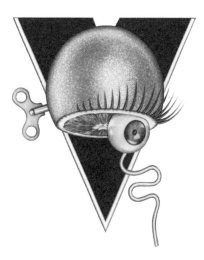

SCI-FI & FANTASY

> "We shall drink to our partnership. Do you like gin? It is my only weakness."
>
> —Ernest Thesiger (as Doctor Pretorius)
> in *The Bride of Frankenstein*

Hope your passport's up-to-date, because we're heading out of this world (not to mention back to the future) in a section that features more dinosaurs than the Natural History Museum and twice the aliens of a Roswell house party. The bad news: A few of these allegedly classic films now play like B-movie horrors, and not the intentional kind. The good news? In space, no one can hear you burp. Prepare to be teleported to planet Tipsy faster than a speeding fanboy.

HARRY POTTER AND THE GIMLET OF FIRE

HARRY POTTER AND THE GOBLET OF FIRE (2005) DIRECTED BY MIKE NEWELL

Smack-dab in the middle of an eight-part film series that took over ten years to film (and took home nearly $8 billion), this was the first *Potter* picture that was dark enough to warrant a PG-13 rating. Now in his fourth year at Hogwarts, our hero Harry becomes an unwitting (and underage) contestant in a treacherous tournament between three neighboring European magic schools. Stick around for the credits of this particular *Potter*, and you'll see a "No dragons were harmed in the making of this movie" gag in the credits—which is more than can be said for any beginner Muggle attempting to make our fiery hooch. (Don't worry, there are two versions of the recipe so that beginner wizards can wave their wands, as well.)

2 ounces gin

1 ounce lime juice

½ ounce simple syrup (page 25)

Beginner's version: Combine all the ingredients with ice in a shaker. Shake well and strain into a cocktail glass (or, of course, a goblet).

Advanced version: After you've completed the above steps, light the tip of a cinnamon stick on fire and then blow it out immediately, incense-style. Wave the stick over the glass, like a ceremonial spell, to give the drink a slightly smoky taste.

A CLOCKWORK ORANGE JULIUS

A CLOCKWORK ORANGE (1971) DIRECTED BY STANLEY KUBRICK

Back when the MPAA ratings board put the "X" in sex, *A Clockwork Orange* had the unusual distinction of being both banned in Britain for nearly thirty years and also nominated for a Best Picture BAFTA (basically the British Oscars). Never a director to shy away from scandalous subjects (this was from the guy who adapted *Lolita* for the screen, after all), Kubrick took an unblinking look into the psychological reprogramming of ultra-violent hoodlums in a dystopian England and was subsequently implicated in copycat murder cases throughout the seventies. Now seen as a seminal-if-schizophrenic morality tale on the dangers of a totalitarian government, *Clockwork* will have you counting back to your own delinquent days with a sloshed twist on a shopping-mall classic.

3 ounces frozen orange juice concentrate

2 ounces vodka

1 ounce whole milk

½ ounce triple sec

1 teaspoon granulated sugar

Combine all the ingredients in a shaker and shake well. Dump the whole thing into a highball glass, drink with an orange silly straw, and resist the urge to TP the neighbors' houses.

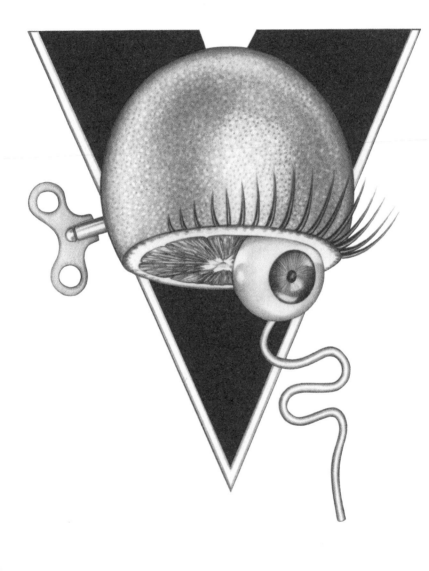

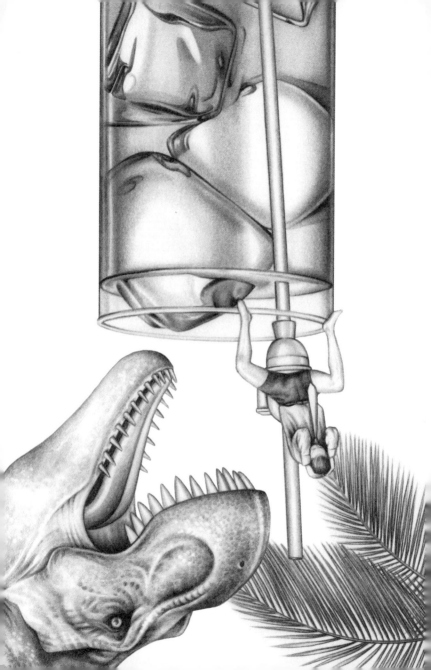

JURASSIC PORT

Wait, an overrun theme park that *isn't* Disney World on spring break? *Jurassic Park* was the brainchild of bestselling novelist Michael Crichton as seen through the wide-lens vision of Steven Spielberg, whose track record for telling humane stories starring inhuman life forms remains unparalleled. Here, the director revolutionized just how jaw-droppingly realistic a forty-foot computerized dinosaur could look (and still looks, decades later), sending theatergoers under their seats—and back for multiple sequels. Get ready for lines around the block when you make our cracked-egg cocktail. It's a scream.

1½ ounces rye whiskey
¾ ounce lemon juice
¾ ounce simple syrup (page 25)
½ ounce port wine
½ egg white

Combine all the ingredients in a shaker and dry shake for 10 seconds. Add a handful of ice and shake well. Strain over fresh ice in a rocks glass, find a secure location, and never forget: If dinosaurs can open doors, they can certainly steal a drink.

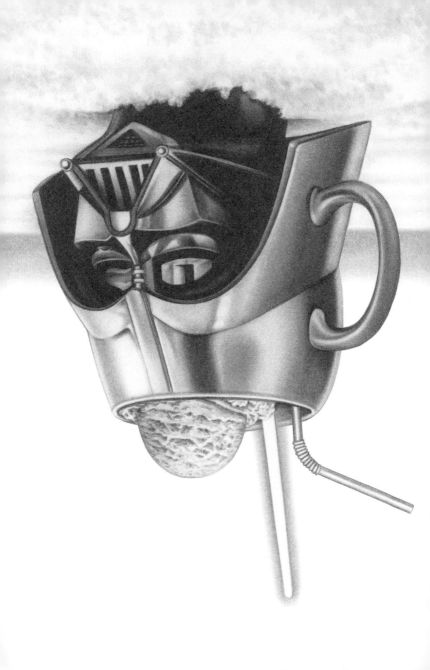

STAR WARS: THE EMPIRE LIKES JACK

STAR WARS EPISODE V: THE EMPIRE STRIKES BACK (1980)
DIRECTED BY IRVIN KERSHNER

In the second installment of this touchstone series, "World's Worst Dad" Darth Vader chases unsuspecting son Luke Skywalker across an entire galaxy—and not to hug it out; their saber-swinging showdown is one of the fiercest fights ever filmed. Though now considered so culturally significant as to feel inevitable, *Empire* was initially struck by struggles: miserable weather on location in Norway (hello, Hoth!), challenges in designing the then-state-of-the-art extra-special effects, and a director who'd never before handled a big-time budget. (It all worked out though, to the tune of half a billion bucks.) Tip your helmet to a dark-versus-light libation that's hiding its own sweet secrets.

8 ounces root beer

1 teaspoon vanilla extract

2 ounces Jack Daniel's

1 scoop vanilla ice cream

Combine the root beer and vanilla in a mug and stir. Add the Jack Daniels and ice cream. May the heavy pour be with you.

CLOSE ENCOUNTERS
OF THE SLURRED KIND

CLOSE ENCOUNTERS OF THE THIRD KIND (1977) DIRECTED BY STEVEN SPIELBERG

Released in the wake of Spielberg's massive hit *Jaws* and catching the sci-fi tailwinds of a little thing called *Star Wars*, *Close Encounters* found success of the mountainous kind—despite blowing its budget and landing as quite a gamble. (The concept of friendly space creatures was revolutionary at the time.) The film stars Richard Dreyfuss in an obsessive performance for which he famously (read: *shamelessly*) campaigned to get cast, with Melinda Dillon in an Oscar-nominated turn as the mother of a kidnapped-to-the-cosmos kiddo. Jealous? Get out of town with our otherworldly beer cocktail that'll have you feeling abducted—by deliciousness!

> 2 ounces tequila
>
> 1 ounce grapefruit juice
>
> 4 ounces UFO Hefeweizen beer
>
> Club soda, to fill

Combine the tequila and grapefruit juice in a shaker and dry shake for a few seconds or until you spot a strange object in the sky—whichever comes first. Pour into a pint glass, add the beer, and fill to the top with club soda.

DAIQ' TO THE FUTURE

BACK TO THE FUTURE (1985) DIRECTED BY ROBERT ZEMECKIS

Not only 1985's top-grossing film about what it would be like to date your own mother, *Back to the Future* was also 1985's top-grossing film *period*, skidding into multiplexes everywhere with Oedipal overtones and teenage hormones. Michael J. Fox gives a timeless performance as an era-hopping slacker whose wacky-haired sidekick (Christopher Lloyd in eccentric Einstein mode) inadvertently wraps Marty up in a Libyan terrorist mishap that sends him thirty years into the past. Time stands still with our Tang-fueled cocktail that'll keep you ticking through further *Future* installments.

Tang powder, for cocktail rim

2 ounces dark rum

1 ounce lime juice

¾ ounce simple syrup (page 25)

2 strawberries, halved

Rim a chilled cocktail glass in Tang powder (page 18) and set aside. Combine all the ingredients with ice in a shaker. Shake well and double-strain into the cocktail glass. (Just don't drink and drive—*especially* not daiquiris and DeLoreans.)

INDIANA JONES AND THE SHIRLEY TEMPLE OF DOOM

INDIANA JONES AND THE TEMPLE OF DOOM (1984)
DIRECTED BY STEVEN SPIELBERG

Prequel *Temple of Doom* traded out some of *Raiders of the Lost Ark's* intellect for twice its twists, including a celebrated chase sequence that finds Indy on a loopy underground train track. If you like your action stars rescuing child slaves from cultish clutches, accompanied by wise-cracking kid sidekicks, and getting the daffy dame at the end of the day, then *Doom* is the Indy for you. Of course, it's all set in a culturally questionable Hindu temple, so this one goes down best with a buzz. Start your night off the way this flick opened: with a splashy Shanghai Shirley Temple in honor of a quirky anything-goes kickoff.

> 1½ ounces tequila
> 4 ounces ginger ale
> 1 ounce lychee juice
> 1½ ounces pomegranate juice
> 1 peeled lychee wedge, for garnish
> Gummy snake (or worm), for garnish

Pour the tequila over ice in a highball glass. One at a time, add the ginger ale, lychee juice, and pomegranate juice. Garnish with the wedge of lychee—and drop in a gummy snake, if you dare.

BLADE RUMMER

BLADE RUNNER (1982) DIRECTED BY RIDLEY SCOTT

A noir detective tale filtered through the smoggy neon of a dystopian Los Angeles, *Blade Runner* cast Harrison Ford as a retired cop who dons the badge again to hunt down a few delinquent bad boys. Good luck finding them, however: In the future, man has created "replicants" who look just like us. Originally deemed too sleepy by audiences who liked their sci-fi served fast, *Blade* has since cut a path as a sleeper hit—due in part to a handful of director's cut releases, the most recent of which found Ridley Scott nixing most of Ford's narration and trusting today's audiences to fill in the pieces. Shake up your own slow night with this one-and-only recipe you'll be cloning into the distant future. Seconds, everyone?

1 orange slice

1 pineapple wedge

1 cherry

1 ounce spiced rum

1 ounce light rum

1 ounce raspberry liqueur

1 ounce crème de banane liqueur

Muddle the fruits in a shaker. Add the remaining ingredients and ice to the shaker. Shake vigorously—and then drink right out of the metal canister for a futuristic freeze.

LONG ISLAND E.T.

E.T. (1982) DIRECTED BY STEVEN SPIELBERG

The rare outer-space saga that favors love over laser beams, Spielberg's extra-special terrestrial was history's top-grossing film for over a decade—till the director's own pack of dinosaurs stomped all over his record, that is. You'd have to be from Mars to remain dry-eyed during this boy-meets-alien tale, which features a young Drew Barrymore as the little sister of lead Henry Thomas—whose weepy audition tape for "Elliott" is floating around online and really has to be seen to be believed. One of the movie's more memorable sequences finds Elliott suddenly inspired to kiss a girl during science class. Do your own chemistry experiment with this eighties take on a kitchen-sink cocktail.

> ¾ ounce light rum
> ¾ ounce vodka
> ¾ ounce gin
> ¾ ounce tequila blanco
> ¾ ounce triple sec
> ½ ounce lemon juice
> ½ ounce orange juice
> '80s-era cola (like Tab), to fill

Combine all the ingredients (except for the cola) in a shaker and dry shake briefly. Dump the whole thing over fresh ice in a Collins glass and fill to the top with the cola. Now chase with a handful of Reese's Pieces.

INVASION OF THE TODDY SNATCHERS

INVASION OF THE BODY SNATCHERS (1956) DIRECTED BY DON SIEGEL

A B-movie mainstay that's surprisingly still suspenseful today, *Invasion* proved compelling enough to inspire three subsequent remakes. In the black-and-white original (and still the best), a small-town California doctor returns from vacation to find the neighbors *looking* normal but acting, well, weird—almost as if they've been switched out for ultra-boring versions of themselves. The film's themes resonated with a paranoid 1950s public wary of creepy communist conformity. On your next restless night, try this sleep-inducing tonic that features an eerily delicious assortment of pods and seeds.

3 ounces hot water

1 ounce bourbon

1 ounce pear brandy

¾ ounce lemon juice

1 tablespoon honey

2 clove studs

Star anise pod

Cinnamon stick, for garnish

Pour the water into a mug and set aside. Combine all the remaining ingredients (except for the cinnamon stick) in a shaker and dry shake. Add to the mug and garnish with the cinnamon stick. Beware of drink-snatchers!

MOVIE MUNCHIES

> "Bad table manners, my dear Gigi,
> have broken up more households
> than infidelity."
>
> —Isabel Jeans (as Aunt Alicia) in *Gigi*

When your head is pounding and your stomach is growling, hit pause and head to the kitchen! Though some movies should never have spawned a sequel, let alone two (did you know there's a *Home Alone 3*?—because, there is!), your guests will be begging for seconds after sampling this bevy of bites inspired by horror films and buddy comedies alike. Remember: The camera only adds ten pounds if it's pointed at you. Phones off, remotes down, and forks out!

THE SILENCE OF THE LAMB BURGERS

THE SILENCE OF THE LAMBS (1991) DIRECTED BY JONATHAN DEMME

The first horror film to take home the Best Picture Oscar, this little lamb didn't always seem like a killer idea: Director Jonathan Demme was best known for the comedy *Married to the Mob* (starring Michelle Pfeiffer, whom Demme initially wanted to headline *Silence*). Even Anthony Hopkins wasn't the first choice to play conniving cannibal Hannibal Lecter—a performance that now tops many a "scariest villain ever" list. Keep on the lights for a fava-bean lamb burger that's best enjoyed *before* watching the film. Hope you can stomach it!

Makes 4 burgers

Fava Bean Purée

1 (15-ounce) can fava beans

1 small potato (like red or fingerling), peeled and diced

½ cup crumbled feta cheese

2 tablespoons extra virgin olive oil

Burgers

1 pound ground lamb

1 tablespoon fresh thyme, coarsely chopped

1 tablespoon fresh parsley, coarsely chopped

1 garlic clove, peeled and minced

Salt and pepper, to taste

Preheat a grill. Drain the beans and purée all the ingredients in a food processor until they are blended but still chunky. Spoon into a small bowl and set aside.

Combine the burger ingredients together in a bowl and then form four loose burgers. Grill on each side between 3 and 4 minutes.

Top the burgers with the fava bean purée and serve on a bed of lettuce, or between your favorite non-human buns. Serve with a glass of Chianti.

GRILLERS IN THE MIST

GORILLAS IN THE MIST (1988) DIRECTED BY MICHAEL APTED

Dian Fossey was a lifelong animal lover from Kentucky when, in the sixties, she became inspired to study the mountain gorillas of Rwanda—whose disappearance at the hands of poachers emboldened Fossey to spend nearly two decades fighting for their survival. Sigourney Weaver's portrayal of Fossey in *Gorillas in the Mist* proved bountiful for the actress: In 1988, she took home Golden Globes for her roles in both *Gorillas* and *Working Girl*. You'll go ape sh*t for this gorilla-ready dessert that ends on a far sweeter note than Fossey's own story. Her murder in Africa, shortly after her memoir was acquired for the film adaptation, remains an unsolved, misty-eyed mystery to this day.

Makes 4 servings

2 bananas

1½ tablespoons light brown sugar

1 tablespoon salted butter, melted

Preheat a grill (ideally outdoors, in a jungle). Peel the bananas and slice them lengthwise and then across their middles to end up with 8 pieces. In a small bowl, combine the sugar and butter with a spoon and then coat the banana pieces. Grill them over medium-high heat between 2 and 4 minutes per side. Remove from the heat and let cool slightly before serving plain or with ice cream.

THE BREAKFAST
CEREAL CLUB

THE BREAKFAST CLUB (1985) DIRECTED BY JOHN HUGHES

Released at the low heights of eighties gross-out comedies, *The Breakfast Club* was auteur John Hughes's standout tribute to troubled suburban teens, and starred a "Brat Pack" of faces who became near-instant cultural icons. Named for the breakfast-hour detention served by five seemingly stereotypical students, the film deftly explores the pressures and crises of adolescence. After Hughes's debut with *Sixteen Candles*, it also solidified him as the poet laureate of teen angst. Our five-ingredient breakfast cereal mix is perfect for any jock, princess, criminal, outcast, or brainiac—*if* you can make it out of the kitchen without finishing it yourself, that is.

Makes one "popcorn bowl" of snack mix

4 cups unsweetened rice or wheat cereal
  (like Chex)

1 cup salted cashews

½ cup (1 stick) salted butter, melted

1 tablespoon hot sauce

2 teaspoons garlic salt

Preheat the oven to 325°F. Mix the cereal and cashews together in a large bowl and set aside. Combine the remaining ingredients in a small bowl and drizzle over the cereal and nuts, stirring to coat. Cover a baking sheet with the snack mix, stir occasionally while baking for about 15 minutes, or until lightly toasted. Let cool and serve in a large bowl—or a Ziploc baggy, if you're heading to detention.

LIFE OF PIE

LIFE OF PI (2012) DIRECTED BY ANG LEE

Leave it to Ang Lee, who proved his technical chops with *Crouching Tiger, Hidden Dragon* and his sensitive side with *Brokeback Mountain*, to helm a 3D adaptation of Yann Martel's tricky oceanic novel. Get to the galley for a vegetarian potpie inspired by the flavors of India.

Makes 4 servings

4 tablespoons (½ stick) unsalted butter

2 small onions, peeled and finely chopped

2 garlic cloves, peeled and minced

2 tablespoons curry powder

½ teaspoon turmeric powder

½ teaspoon paprika

½ teaspoon garlic salt

2 medium potatoes, peeled and diced

1 medium carrot, peeled and diced

1½ cups green peas, fresh or frozen

½ cup cilantro, minced

Salt and pepper, to taste

1 sheet puff pastry, thawed

Melt the butter in a large pot over medium heat. Add the onion and cook about 10 minutes, stirring occasionally, until golden. Add the garlic and stir for 30 seconds. Add the seasonings and stir occasionally for another 5 minutes.

Preheat the oven to 375°F.

Add the potatoes and carrot and a cup of water and cover the pot, stirring occasionally, for about 15 minutes, or until the potatoes can be pierced with a fork. Stir in the peas and cilantro and add salt and pepper to taste. Transfer everything to a 3-quart greased baking dish and place the puff pastry on top. Slice four vents into the pastry and bake for about 20 to 25 minutes, or until the top is golden.

Remove from the oven and let cool for about 10 minutes before enjoying. And save enough for your shipmates!

TRUE GRITS

Based on the great American novel that first inspired a film adaptation in 1969 (starring Western stalwart John Wayne), this 2010 version surpassed box-office projections—perhaps in part owing to its rare-for-the-Coen-brothers PG-13 rating. In *True Grit*, a stubborn girl hires a drunk, eye patch–wearing U.S. marshall to head into Indian country and help her avenge the murder of her father. With a cast headed by then-unknown thirteen-year-old Hailee Steinfeld, *True Grit* lassoed in ten Oscar nominations, though it went home empty-handed. Prep for your next road trip with a Texas grits recipe that'll have you ready for an adventure—or a nap.

Makes 4 servings

1 cup instant grits

2 eggs

1 cup grated white cheddar cheese

4 tablespoons (½ stick) salted butter

2 teaspoons hot sauce

1 teaspoon salt

1 teaspoon pepper

2 jalapeños, seeded and diced

Preheat the oven to 300°F. Safely store your rifle and then prepare the grits on a stovetop as instructed on the box. Beat the eggs in a small bowl and add them and the remaining ingredients to the grits. Stir well and transfer the grits to a 2-quart greased casserole dish. Bake for 45 to 50 minutes, or until the top of the casserole is lightly browned. Remove from the oven and let cool for about 10 minutes before serving.

BONUS!
DRINKING GAMES

Take a shot every time:

Showgirls takes itself too seriously.

Dick Van Dyke attempts a Cockney accent in
Mary Poppins

Somebody slow-claps during any movie
from the eighties.

You get up to pee during the three-hour-long
Gandhi.

You sob during *Up*. Take two shots if it's within the
first five minutes.

Ben Stein says "Bueller?" in *Ferris Bueller's Day Off*.

You know a line in *Clue*—especially Madeline
Kahn's "Flames . . . on the side of my face" speech.

Robin Williams says "Good Morning, Vietnam!"
in *Good Morning, Vietnam*.

Somebody says the f-word in *Pulp Fiction*.

Anybody says "Beetlejuice" in *Beetlejuice*.

George W. Bush smirks in *Fahrenheit 9/11*.

Judy Garland's wig changes length in *The Wizard of Oz*.

The villain of any movie finally corners the hero,
and instead of killing him, delivers a four-minute
monologue.

You roll your eyes when *The Notebook* is on
TV—and then "accidentally" end up watching
the entire thing.

FORMULAS FOR METRIC CONVERSIONS

Ounces to grams. . . . . multiply ounces by 28.35

Pounds to grams . . . . multiply pounds by 453.5

Cups to liters . . . . multiply cups by .24

Fahrenheit to centigrade . . . . subtract 32 from
Fahrenheit, multiply by 5,
and divide by 9

U.S.	Metric	
⅛ tsp.	0.6 ml	
¼ tsp.	1.2 ml	
½ tsp.	2.5 ml	
¾ tsp.	3.7 ml	
1 tsp.	5 ml	
1½ tsp.	7.4 ml	
2 tsp.	10 ml	
1 Tbsp.	15 ml	
1½ Tbsp.	22 ml	
2 Tbsp. (⅛ cup)	30 ml	1 fl. oz
3 Tbsp.	45 ml	
¼ cup	59 ml	2 fl. oz
⅓ cup	79 ml	
½ cup	118 ml	4 fl. oz
⅔ cup	158 ml	
¾ cup	178 ml	6 fl. oz
1 cup	237 ml	8 fl. oz
1¼ cups	300 ml	
1½ cups	355 ml	
1¾ cups	425 ml	
2 cups (1 pint)	500 ml	16 fl. oz
3 cups	725 ml	
4 cups (1 quart)	.95 liters	32 fl. oz
16 cups (1 gallon)	3.8 liters	128 fl. oz

Oven Temperatures

Degrees Fahrenheit	Degrees Centigrade	British Gas Marks
200°	93°	—
250°	120°	½
275°	140°	1
300°	150°	2
325°	165°	3
350°	175°	4
375°	190°	5
400°	200°	6
450°	230°	8

Metric Equivalents for Weight

U.S.	Metric
1 oz	28 g
2 oz	57 g
3 oz	85 g
4 oz	113 g
5 oz	142 g
6 oz	170 g
7 oz	198 g
8 oz	227 g
16 oz (1 lb.)	454 g
2.2 lbs.	1 kilogram

U.S.	Metric
2 tsp.	10 g
1 Tbsp.	15 g
1½ Tbsp.	22.5 g
2 Tbsp. (1 oz)	27 g
3 Tbsp.	42 g
4 Tbsp.	56 g
4 oz (1 stick)	110 g
8 oz (2 sticks)	220 g

Metric Equivalents for Length

U.S.	Metric
¼ inch	.65 cm
½ inch	1.25 cm
1 inch	2.50 cm
2 inches	5.00 cm
3 inches	6.00 cm
4 inches	8.00 cm
5 inches	11.00 cm
6 inches	15.00 cm
7 inches	18.00 cm
8 inches	20.00 cm
9 inches	23.00 cm
12 inches	30.50 cm
15 inches	38.00 cm

Acknowledgments

Barely sober thanks to: everyone at Running Press, especially Jordana Tusman, Susan Weinberg, Kristin Kiser, Josh McDonnell, Seta Zink, and Cassie Drumm (you too, Allison Devlin); artist-from-Heaven Lauren Mortimer; eagle-eyed copy editor Joelle Herr and proofreader Diana Drew; Cheri Steinkellner, for being the best first audience on the page and beyond; friends and followers on Twitter, Instagram, and Facebook (I'm at @TimFederle) who pitched many of the puns contained within; Ann Louden, Texas's best cheerleader; my cocktail guru Cody Goldstein; my agent Brenda Bowen and everyone at Sanford J. Greenburger Associates; and readers of *Tequila Mockingbird* and *Hickory Daiquiri Dock*, for making this ongoing gig so damn fun. Lastly, and mostly, thank you to the many moviemakers whose work inspired my own.

INDEX

E

D

F

Y

Z

HAVING A MOVIE NIGHT?

THROWING A CINEMATIC PARTY?

DRINKING . . . ALONE?

Snap a photo of your favorite drink and tag it on Twitter and Instagram with #GoneWithTheGin to connect with author Tim Federle at @TimFederle.

Be Kind, Rewind, and Read Responsibly!